The Girl Who Married a Ghost

and Other Tales from the North American Indian

"His power was very great" (page 104)

The Girl Who Married a Ghost
and Other Tales from the North American Indian

Collected, and with photographs, by
Edward S. Curtis | Edited by John Bierhorst

Four Winds Press · New York

Library of Congress Cataloging in Publication Data

Curtis, Edward S.   1868–1952.
The girl who married a ghost and other tales from
The North American Indian.

Contents: From the Northwest coast: The girl who
married a ghost. The dance of the spirit monster.—From
California: Asleep-by-the-stream.—From the Plains:
The deserted children. Fox and the bears. [etc.]
1. Indians of North America—Legends. [1. Indians of
North America—Legends]   I.   Title.
E98.F6C93   1977   398.2'097 [398.2]   77–21515
ISBN 0–590–07505–5

Published by Four Winds Press
A Division of Scholastic Magazines, Inc., New York, N.Y.
Copyright © 1978 by John Bierhorst
All rights reserved
Printed in the United States of America
Library of Congress Catalog Card Number: 77–21515
Designed by Jane Byers Bierhorst
1 2 3 4 5   82 81 80 79 78

Foreword

Edward Curtis's Indian tales are among the relatively few — like those of H. R. Schoolcraft and George Bird Grinnell — that succeed in bringing authentic Indian source materials into the mainstream of popular literature. Though they preserve the strangeness of a different way of thinking, these stories were translated with just enough freedom to make the strange seem comprehensible. Through them the English-speaking reader, or listener, can enter an imaginary world that might otherwise remain permanently closed.

Like Schoolcraft a half-century before him, Curtis conceived a massive project for saving the remnants of what he believed to be a vanishing race. His completed work, entitled *The North American Indian,* filled twenty volumes and covered all the major tribal divisions west of the Mississippi. Published over a period of twenty-three years beginning in 1907, it included detailed descriptions of tribal life, some three hundred and fifty traditional tales, and over two thousand of Curtis's own, superbly romantic, soft-toned photographs.

Curtis enjoyed considerable popularity while his project was under way. He was often the subject of newspaper articles and was in demand as a lecturer. When his great work was finished, however, it all but disappeared. Only five hundred sets of *The North American Indian* were printed, and these so sumptuously that the few institutions able to purchase them have kept them hidden away in rare-book rooms.

At the time of his death, in 1952, and for a decade or more thereafter, Edward Curtis was a relatively obscure figure. But in 1971 a new wave of enthusiasm was set in motion by a profoundly influential exhibit of his photographs at the Morgan Library in New York. Since then his work has been widely discussed and exhibited, and several noteworthy collections of the again-famous pictures have been published, including the jumbo *Portraits from North American Indian Life* (Outerbridge and Lazard) and the unusually rich-toned *North American Indians* (Aperture) — yet, until now, no anthology of Curtis's tales.

The truth is that Curtis's photographs, though generally regarded as portraits from "life," have more in common with the tales, or myths, than they do with the day-to-day lives of the people who served as their subjects. One purpose of the present volume is to reveal this link between image and myth.

It must be kept in mind that Curtis was an ardent, lifelong collector of fictional narratives. Neither Schoolcraft nor Grinnell recorded nearly so many. For sheer bulk, his output is rivaled only by such indefatigable fieldworkers as Franz Boas and Alfred Kroeber, whose conception of the Indian tale as a literary form, however, was considerably less vivid than Curtis's. If the mantle of the brothers Grimm can be said to have passed from the Old World to the New, it must have settled upon the shoulders of Curtis and his faithful assistant, W. E. Myers (whose intuitive linguistic skills are said to have been startling).

It is perhaps worth mentioning that the nine tales in this book have been chosen in order to preserve on a small scale both the geographical range and the folkloristic variety of the whole work. At least one story is presented from each of the major regions that Curtis covered, and the story types include a sacred origin-myth ("How the World Was Saved"), a decidedly nonsacred campfire yarn ("The Woman Dressed Like a Man"), a ghost story ("The Girl Who Married a Ghost"), and a trickster tale ("Fox and the Bears").

While working in the field with native storytellers, Curtis used interpreters. The stories were taken down in shorthand, by Myers, and later reworked, by Curtis, into a smooth English version. Though he was a competent writer, Curtis, like Schoolcraft, often wrote hastily, and with this in mind I have made numerous minor revisions in editing the tales given here. (A few passages have been completely retold.) For the most part, however, the wording is Curtis's.

As for the accompanying photographs, only a few, such as the illustration of the Spirit Monster (page 27) and the one of the Fire God (page 91), were originally published in context with the stories. The majority were inserted several or even many pages distant from the passages to which I have here matched them. In studying Curtis's work in its entirety, one finds that the narrative incidents and the photographic images reinforce each other constantly, sometimes in a general way, sometimes with exquisite specificity. Once again, in making my choices, I have tried to convey on a small scale the spirit of the work as a whole.

As has often been pointed out, many if not most of the pictures were carefully staged, the actual shooting being preceded by hours or even days of preparation. Through it all, Curtis had the full cooperation of his Indian subjects, who obviously sympathized with his aims. Inasmuch as they worked with him to create the effects both he and they desired, it can be said with justification that the pictures, like the stories, are true to the Indians' own vision of themselves.

Grateful acknowledgment is made to my wife, Jane Byers Bierhorst, and to my daughter, Alice, who assisted me in the selection of the photographs; and to the staff of the Vassar College Library — especially Frances Goudy — who permitted me to use their copy of *The North American Indian* for my research.

J.B.

Contents

FROM THE NORTHWEST COAST

The Girl Who Married a Ghost | 5

The Dance of the Spirit Monster | 21

FROM CALIFORNIA

Asleep-by-the-Stream | 35

FROM THE PLAINS

The Deserted Children | 45

Fox and the Bears | 54

FROM THE NORTH WOODS

The Woman Dressed Like a Man | *61*

FROM THE SOUTHWEST

The Dirty Bride | *73*
How the World Was Saved | *81*

FROM ALASKA

The Lost Boys | *99*

A Note About the Making of This Book | *112*
Books By and About Edward Curtis | *114*

Illustrations

"His power was very great" | frontispiece

"there lived a rich man who had three daughters" | 6

"especially the eldest, who was the most beautiful of all" | 7

"a great house" | 10

"as much a person of the spirit land as of the earth" | 15

"when darkness fell, the ghosts came for her and the child" | 19

"at the mouth of the river, where they had a small hut" | 22–3

" 'If you can show me where my son is, I will take you to my house' " | 27

"he was wearing the mask of the spirit monster" | 29

"He did not know where he was or how he had come there." | 37

"Yet there he was. He had reappeared." | 40

"the parents were moving to a new camp . . ." | 46

"... and had left the children on purpose" | 47

"the tribe increased and their hearts were good" | 52–3

"He howled with pain." | 55

"She said, 'Little boys, give me a drink.' " | 65

"Then the young man went in." | 68

"Each day he would make an offering to the gods" | 74

"they all wished to marry this handsome boy" | 76–7

"she revealed her true self" | 79

"when the day grew warm, she would go down to a stream" | 83

" 'Are you afraid, my younger brother?' " | 85

"there before them stood the Fire God" | 91

"The people were no longer afraid to travel from place
   to place." | 94

"in a house at the edge of the sea" | 100

"Close by were women cutting meat." | 103

"her power was the greatest of all" | 106

"and dressed them in fine clothing" | 107

From the Northwest Coast

*Few North American tribes were as fortunate as those that
lived along the Pacific shore from Oregon to southern Alaska.
There the waters teemed with fish and seals — in such
quantities that a year's supply of food could be gotten with
little effort. In villages up and down the coast were families
owning rich hoards of dried salmon, canoes, blankets, robes,
copper ornaments, and carved dishes. In the winter, when
work was done, they enjoyed a season of leisure, playing host
at elaborate ceremonies over which they presided in the
manner of lords. Their sons and daughters were regarded as
"princes" and "princesses." The daughter of the rich chief in
"The Girl Who Married a Ghost" was such a princess. Her
story is from the Nisqualli tribe of southern Washington. The
story that follows it, "The Dance of the Spirit Monster," is
from the Kwakiutl of Canada. It tells how the winter
ceremonial, or Winter Dance, was first performed. Both
stories are myths, supposed to have been handed down from
ancient times.*

The Girl Who Married a Ghost

In the ancient days, on a sheltered bay not far from the ocean, there lived a rich man who had three daughters.

This man was a chief and well known for his thrift and his strong character, but he was equally famous for the beauty of his daughters, especially the eldest, who was the most beautiful of all. From far and near came parents and other relatives of eager young men, hoping the chief might consent to the marriage of one or another of his daughters.

"there lived a rich man who
had three daughters"

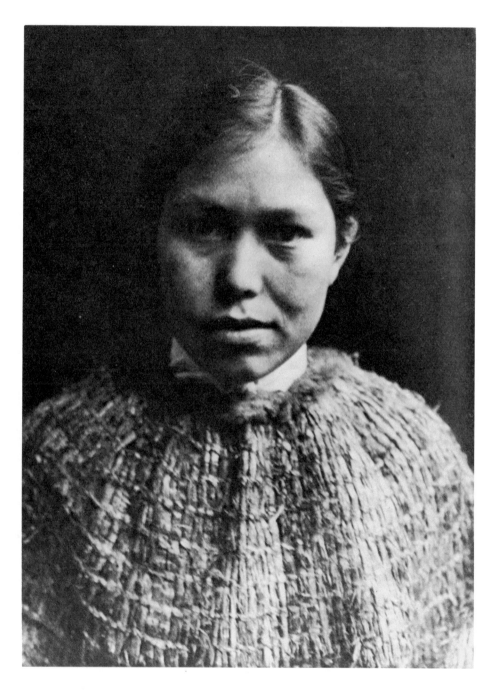

*"especially the eldest, who was the
most beautiful of all"*

But to all their promises of lavish gifts, the old man turned a deaf ear. He was happy with his family just as it was, and as for money, he needed no more than he had already.

Again and again he said no, until at last he aroused the hatred and ill will of the neighboring villages. It became an openly expressed wish that something dreadful might happen to the stubborn chief. And once, when he declined to give up his eldest daughter, the visitors angrily denounced him, saying they hoped that ghosts would come and buy her and carry her off to the land of the dead.

To this the old man gave no heed. But not long afterward, from out on the ocean one night, came the sound of many voices singing gay, rollicking songs. As the sound drew nearer, the chief and his family saw many canoes filled with people — a bridegroom's wedding party.

When they had landed and made known their desire, so great were their numbers and so rich their gifts that the chief was unable to refuse, and without hesitation he gave his consent to the marriage of his eldest daughter to a handsome, richly dressed young man.

The wedding ceremony lasted the greater part of the

night, yet long before dawn the visitors, accompanied by the bride, set off in their canoes and paddled away into the darkness, singing exultantly. Out onto the ocean they paddled, until they could no longer be seen or heard. Where they were headed, or who they truly were, the chief and his family did not know, yet strangely they felt no misgivings.

The wedding guests paddled on and on — until suddenly a dark, mysterious land loomed up before them. They drew quickly to shore, hauled their canoes onto the beach, and went off in various directions. Although it was not yet daylight, the girl found that she could see without difficulty. Everywhere there were groups of people playing games, some gambling with marked bones, others with wooden discs, some playing shinny, and others shooting arrows at a rolling hoop. As far as she could see there were people, all boisterously happy.

She followed her husband to a great house, in which he and many others dwelled. Side by side on the raised platform around the base of the walls slept great numbers of children. The portion of the house to which her husband

"a great house"

led her was screened off by broad rush mats. Soft mats and many blankets covered their bed. It was time to sleep, her husband said. And indeed, after the long night of excitement and travel she was glad to retire.

When the young wife awoke, the sun was already high in the sky, but not a sound greeted her. She thought this odd, recalling the crowds of people she had seen the night before, and turned to look at her husband, whose head rested on her arm. To her horror she found herself gazing into the empty sockets of a grinning skull. What had been a handsome young man was now a skeleton.

Without moving her arm she raised herself on her elbow and peered about. The rows of sleeping children were now rows of whitened bones. Was she dreaming? The bedding that had been so fine was now dirty and old and worn to shreds. The great house was blackened by smoke and almost ready to fall. Only her own clothing remained as it had been when she went to sleep.

Slowly it dawned on her that she had been trapped by some evil magic, and she began to think of escape. She feared to look again at what had been her husband, nor dared to disturb it. Yet she must escape. Slowly, carefully, she moved her arm until it was free, and as the skull slipped from the crook of her elbow it dropped upon the blanket and turned on its side.

She arose, dressed hurriedly, and began to pick her way among the bones and the musty utensils and clothing. When she reached the doorway, she was greeted by another gruesome sight. Strewn about in groups were endless numbers of skeletons — bones, everywhere bones, up and down the shore as far as she could see — in all sorts of positions and still at the various games the people had been playing when daylight had overtaken them.

But the sight of the water gave her hope. She would take a canoe and paddle away, and eventually she would find her home. So thick were the bones on the ground that occasionally she had to push them aside with her foot to avoid walking on them. She could see the prows of canoes above the line of beach gravel, and toward these she carefully threaded her way.

But alas, she found that the boats were old, weather-beaten, decayed, grown over with moss, and full of holes.

One after another she pushed them into the water, only to see them fill and sink. Overcome by despair, she collapsed on the gravel and sobbed bitterly.

The crying relieved her feelings. She bathed and dried her face, then looked about. Far down the beach, where a point of land jutted into the water, a wisp of smoke curled upward. Somewhat encouraged, she began walking toward it. The bones of the dead lay all about her. But the thought that human life might still exist in this terrifying place, and that she might soon find companionship, emboldened the girl as she plodded along. She became more careless of how she stepped on the bones or moved them aside.

She made her way slowly, however, and the distance was greater than she expected. The sun had already been traveling a considerable time on its downward course before she reached the place where the smoke was rising. When at last she got there, she found a tiny old woman sitting with her back turned, weaving baskets from hair. The girl hesitated, wondering what she should say. "Come, child," said the little woman without turning around. "You are the one they brought down yesterday."

The woman was Screech Owl. As she spoke, she went right on with her work, for she had not been in the least surprised. Being as much a person of the spirit land as of the earth, she passed back and forth whenever she wished and knew everything that happened in either world. She assured the girl that there was nothing to fear and that she was perfectly safe from harm.

"You do not understand," said the little woman. "You do not know where you are or what to do. This is the land of the ghost people. Those who die on earth come here. When you came, it was night on the earth, and that is the time when the ghosts are active. At sunrise they go to sleep. They have no real bodies at night, and by day they lie about as bones. You must do but one thing: sleep when they sleep and wake when they wake, and all will be well for you. Your only mistake is that you woke too soon. You should have slept. All these people whose skeletons you have seen will begin to move at sunset. You had better stay with me until you see."

So the girl spent the rest of the afternoon with Screech

"as much a person of the spirit
land as of the earth"

Owl, learning much about the people among whom she had married. As the sun sank below the horizon and shadows deepened into twilight, the sound of faint voices came from the distance, swelling gradually into great choruses of singing and gleeful shouting. But the ghosts soon noticed that something was wrong and that the bride they had brought home the night before was missing. Knowing that Screech Owl was the only person she might find to keep her company in daylight, they came running down that way. Some of them were furious and waved their arms wildly.

Their anger, the girl soon discovered, was due to the fact that she had wounded many of them on her way from the village to the home of Screech Owl. Every time she had moved a bone she had severely injured a ghost, and where she had pushed aside a whole skeleton, that ghost had died. A threatening crowd surrounded her. Not satisfied with injuring innumerable people, they cried, she had thoughtlessly pushed into the water many fine canoes, which had drifted away on the tide. Worst of all, she had nearly killed her own husband by half twisting off his head.

To all these threats and cries for vengeance Screech Owl replied by scolding the ghosts for their failure to tell the girl who they were and what she must do while living among them. Silenced, the angry ones turned to go, and the girl accompanied them. As they went along, they passed many anxious groups attending to the wounded. Some were beyond help. Others had knees twisted, ribs displaced, arms disjointed, feet missing. Her husband she found recovering from what had seemed an almost fatal injury. From that time on, the girl was careful to do as Screech Owl had advised.

Time passed happily, and one day the young wife gave birth to a baby boy, of whom she was very proud. But the ghosts were troubled by this arrival of a child neither properly a ghost nor a human being. They insisted upon taking the mother and her baby back to her earthly home, and so those who had made up the wedding party again voyaged to the earth.

It was dark when they reached the shore where her people lived, but her parents had heard the distant sound of singing and had built a great fire, which lighted the whole house. They were delighted to see their daughter and her child. A fine baby, a pretty boy, everyone said as they passed him from one to another. Then the ghosts told the child's mother that for twelve days she must not unwrap him on his cradleboard by daylight, or he would change and would have to be returned to ghost land. After this warning, the ghost people silently withdrew.

For eleven days the young mother watched her little boy. Each day she went to the woods to gather moss and cedar bark, which she shredded and used to pad the baby on his cradleboard. On the twelfth day she remained absent a long time, and her mother, curious to see if this child brought from ghost land were like other children, unlaced the wrapping.

Raising the blanket, she was shocked to discover the bones of a little skeleton, and indignantly cast bones and cradleboard out of the house. At that instant the baby's mother began to feel ill. Sensing that something had happened to her child, she hurried home to see what was the matter. When she got there and found the cradleboard on the ground and the little bones scattered in the sunlight, she

*"when darkness fell, the ghosts came
for her and the child"*

flew into a rage and rebuked her mother severely. One more day and she and her child might have lived happily on earth.

As it was, when darkness fell, the ghosts came for her and the child. Before she departed, the young mother told her parents that she would return to earth once more, though not to their home, nor to remain as much as a day, for they had driven her from them.

Just as she had promised, she came again one night with many of her ghost people, and after singing out on the water for a while they paddled away. Neither the girl nor her child was ever seen again. They themselves had at last become ghosts.

From that time on, no living creature has been able to travel to ghost land, nor do we know what the ghosts are doing or what they are saying there. No living creature, that is, but Screech Owl, who still flies back and forth whenever she chooses. She does not reveal herself to us in human form, however, nor will she speak our language, though sometimes at night we may hear her cry or see her shadow above the smoke hole.

The Dance of the Spirit Monster

One evening a hunter and his wife went downstream to fish and landed at the mouth of the river, where they had a small hut. They spent the night. The next morning the man caught some salmon, and his wife cleaned them and laid them on a drying rack under the smoke hole. Again they spent the night.

When it was dark, the woman heard something on the roof. Her husband was snoring. She watched the smoke

"at the mouth of the river, where
they had a small hut"

hole, and seeing a dim shape moving overhead, she nudged her husband and whispered, "There's a man above the smoke hole!" The hunter looked up and caught sight of a person pushing aside the roof mats to get at the drying salmon. His bow lay next to him. Cautiously he strung it, put an arrow on the string, and shot with the full strength of the bow. The person fell backward and slipped off the roof. There was a crash in the brush and the noise of something creeping away.

Early the next morning the hunter went to see what he had shot, and after following the trail a short distance he found the body of a strange creature with great, hanging breasts and a round, protruding mouth. It was a spirit monster. He covered the body and, returning to the hut, said to his wife, "I killed that thing. It was a male spirit-monster. Now we must go home." They paddled up the river to the village, landed, and went into their house.

The morning after their return, a party of men going downriver saw a huge female spirit-monster, wailing on top of a rock in the middle of the stream. They turned back at once and hurried home to report what they had seen, and the hunter whispered to his wife, "That spirit monster is crying for the one I killed!"

There were some reckless young men who wanted to go investigate, but the ones who had just returned warned them: "Don't go near that thing! Its eyes are enormous, they're filled with fire. Its head is as big as a storage chest."

"We'll go anyway," said the young men. "We're not afraid of it." So they got into their canoe and paddled downstream. When they got close to the rock, they asked the spirit monster why she was wailing. "I have lost my son!" she cried. Then they hurried back to the village to warn the people, thinking the monster would come kill someone to avenge the death of her son.

When the warning had been given, an ugly young man, a very sad boy who seldom spoke, got up without a word. In some way he knew that the hunter had killed the spirit monster. He took his paddle and proceeded downstream. He let his canoe drift quite close to the rock before he spoke: "What are you crying about, good one?"

"I have lost my son," she answered. "If you can find him for me, I will make you handsome and rich."

The ugly boy had now backed his canoe right up to the rock, and the monster took hold of it. "Step over the water," he said. And taking but a single step, she strode to the shore. The young man paddled after her and landed. "If you can show me where my son is, I will take you to my house," she said. Then the young man led her to the hut that had been used by the hunter and his wife the day before. Sadly, he entered and looked at the disarranged matting around the smoke hole. Then he came out and followed the trail to where the body lay. The monster reached down and cradled it in her long arms. "Come," she said, "we will go to my home." As she led him along, carrying the body of her dead son, the young man noticed that she no longer wept. Soon they entered a great house.

"Now," she said, "all these things are yours." She pointed to dressed skins and dried mountain-goat meat, and a mask that was just like the face of her son. "With this," she said, "you will become a spirit dancer and dance this winter before all the people of your tribe. He tried on the mask, and she showed him how to dance. Still the boy seemed sad.

Then, starting toward one corner of the room, the spirit

" 'If you can show me where my son is, I
will take you to my house' "

monster said, "Come, see what I will do with my son." In the corner was a round hole, and inside the hole there was water, some of which she sprinkled on her son, and he became alive. This was living water. She told the young man he could have it for his own use. Then she threw some of it on him, and he became handsome. Even so, he was not happy.

"The reason I am sad," he said at last, "is that my mother and father are both dead. Can I bring them back to life?"

"You can if you know where they are," she replied. Then, as she turned to leave, she said, "I must go now to a safe place where no one can harm my son." And with that the spirit monsters departed.

When they had gone, the young man filled a small pouch with the living water, loaded his canoe with as much of the meat and as many of the skins as he could carry, and went home to get his people to help him with larger canoes. They brought back enough food for a great celebration.

Then the young man gave the first Winter Dance. There was much feasting, and many fine skins were distributed as gifts. At the height of the celebration the young man himself disappeared. When he returned, he was wearing

*"he was wearing the mask of
the spirit monster"*

the mask of the spirit monster. He danced the dance that the spirit had taught him, and the people were amazed.

But the hunter who had killed the spirit monster was angry. He argued with the young man. "I killed the spirit monster," he cried. "This dance should be mine. I earned it with blood. You did nothing!"

But the young man retorted, "The spirit gave me this dance. She did not say, 'Take this dance and give it to the one who killed my son.' She gave it to me. It can never be yours."

Then the hunter was ashamed before his tribe. Together with his wife he slipped away, and the two were never seen in the village again.

When the young man had finished dancing, there were other dances, and people sang songs. While they were singing, the boy disappeared a second time. This time he returned with the bodies of his mother and father. He sprinkled them with the living water and saw them sit upright, rub their eyes, and say, "We have slept long!" Then the parents and the boy danced together. The parents were happy. The boy was happy too.

From California

The region now known as California was once inhabited by more than a hundred different tribes, all speaking different languages. Most of these groups were very small, living usually along streams or rivers in tiny villages, many of which had no more than five or six houses. In the north the houses were made of wood, like those of the northwest coast tribes, but smaller and simpler. Although the people took fish from the rivers and went often to the shore to hunt seals or gather shellfish, they seldom ventured out onto the ocean. The sea remained a place of mystery, unknown and possibly dangerous. The little story that follows is a tale about the sea. It comes from the Wiyot of northern California, a tribe now all but extinct, formerly living around Humboldt Bay and as far south as the Eel River.

Asleep-by-the-Stream

On Eel River there lived a boy who never stepped outside
his house. And yet this boy had two sweethearts. All day
long the two girls would stand next to the door, waiting for
a glimpse of the boy inside, and all day long the boy would
sleep. His name was Asleep-by-the-Stream. Day after day
he slept. He never went out at all.

At last the girls grew tired of waiting, and one of them
said, "We'll get a canoe and carry our boy out into it and

take him down the river." So they did. And at the mouth of the river the other girl said, "We might as well bring him out on the ocean." So they carried him through a little bay to the ocean itself and there, far from shore, they put him down on a rock.

People soon knew that the sleepy boy had left his house. The girls were no longer seen at his door. People wondered what had become of him.

After a long while, lying on the rock where the girls had left him, the boy awoke. He did not know where he was or how he had come there. "Somebody must have brought me to this place," he said. Then he began to cry. "How am I going to get back home?"

Late in the afternoon he looked toward the south. It was a clear day. He saw some birds sailing in the still air. He continued to cry. Again he looked south. The birds were larger. They were getting closer.

He kept on crying, but looked again. A person was coming over the water. He cried. He looked again. This time he was certain that what he saw was a man, walking on the water. Still crying, he watched the man. Then he

*"He did not know where he was
or how he had come there."*

said to himself, "I wonder who this is? If he can walk on water, surely I can too. Who can this be that walks on water as though it were land?"

The man climbed up on the rock. He was the one called Gone-Down-to-the-Sea. He asked, "How did you come here?"

"I don't know," said the boy.

"Are you sure you don't know?"

"Yes, I don't know. I've been sleeping all the time. I had two girls who loved me. They stayed about the house while I slept, and I think it may be they who brought me here. But I don't know for sure."

Gone-Down-to-the-Sea said, "I am headed north."

"But do you know how I am going to get home?" asked the sleepy one.

"Yes, sometime you will get home. But now I am going northward to the land of many souls. There is going to be a dance. I am going to see it. You had better come too."

"No," said the boy, "I would like to go with you, but I cannot walk on water."

"Well, follow me. Try it."

He climbed down and walked on the water as if it were land. But the boy was afraid to try it. Again he was urged, and at last he became desperate and said, "I might as well drown as starve here!" So he climbed down and stepped on the water. It was solid under his feet. Then they went northward, and at nightfall they arrived at the place where the dance was to be. The souls had just begun dancing.

The boy was poor, and Gone-Down-to-the-Sea thought, "I will beg something for him. I am a stranger here, and no one knows me. I will be a medicine man and sing beside the fire." So he stood beside the fire and led the singing, and the souls continued their dancing. At the end of the dance, Gone-Down-to-the-Sea addressed them: "I want to see you give presents to this young man. I found him in the ocean, lying on a rock. Give him presents, everybody!"

Then the souls crowded near, and each gave something. In this way the boy became rich.

The next morning Gone-Down-to-the-Sea said to his friend, "I am going home. Come with me. We will walk on land this time." So they started southward. As they traveled along, the boy stopped frequently to rest. After a long while

"Yet there he was. He had reappeared."

they came in sight of the boy's village, and, leaving his friend there, Gone-Down-to-the-Sea went on. Once again the boy stopped to rest.

When the news went about that the sleepy boy had returned, all were astonished, for the girls had told everyone what they had done to him. Yet there he was. He had reappeared. When at last he reached his house, the people gathered around him and asked, "How did you get back? Did you swim ashore?"

"No," he said, "Gone-Down-to-the-Sea led me home."

The two girls, hearing that the one they loved had returned, came immediately to his house to see him. They sat next to the door, one on each side, and looked in. They wanted very much to see him. But he did not wish to see them. He came to the door and put one foot and his head out, and as he stepped through he placed his hands on the heads of the two girls, passing by without looking, and said, "I hope you will become stones."

Then he looked back and saw that they were stones. And there they remained, motionless, outside the door of Asleep-by-the-Stream.

From the Plains

The Indians of the Plains were big-game hunters, whose way of life depended upon the herds of buffalo, elk, and deer that once roamed freely between the Mississippi River and the Rocky Mountains. As the herds moved, so did the people, dragging their tepee poles behind them. "The Deserted Children," from the Gros Ventre of Montana, is the story of a boy and a girl who were left behind when such a move was made. The story that follows it is a trickster tale from the Comanche of Texas. The story makes fun of a well-known funeral custom whereby a dead person's relatives, to display their grief, would cut their hair and rub their bodies with ashes.

The Deserted Children

One day a little boy and his sister, returning from play,
found only smoldering campfires where their village had
been. Deep in the distance the people could still be seen,
traveling farther and farther away. As they hurried to catch
up, the children found a tepee pole that had been dropped
by their parents. "Mother!" they shouted. "Here is one of
your poles!" But the parents were moving to a new camp
and had left the children on purpose, not caring for them,

"the parents were moving to a new camp..."

". . . and had left the children on purpose"

and from far away came the faint answer, "Never mind, you are not my child!"

The sister kept stopping to help her little brother, who was too young to keep going, and the two were soon left far behind. She led him to a thicket and, making him a bed of boughs, left him there to rest while she cut brush and built a small shelter. From then on they lived in this shelter, eating berries and roots gathered by the child-mother. Many summers passed. The children grew older.

One day, as the girl was looking out of their little lodge, she saw a herd of elk going by, and she exclaimed, "Brother, look at the elk! So many!"

The boy was sitting with his head bowed. His eyes were cast downward, because he was now old enough to feel ashamed of living alone with his sister, and without looking up he replied, "Sister, it will do us no good if I look at them."

But she insisted. Then the boy raised his head and looked at the elk, and they all fell dead in their tracks.

The girl went out, skinned and butchered the elk, and carried the flesh and hides into the lodge. Looking at the pile of meat, she said, "I wish this meat were dried," and no sooner were the words out of her mouth than it was all perfectly dried. Lifting a hide and shaking it, she said, "I wish these hides were tanned," and so they were. She spread a number of them on the ground and murmured to herself, "I wish these were sewn into a tepee cover," and behold! there was a fine, large, tepee cover lying where the unsewn skins had been. Later the same day a herd of buffalo appeared, and she cried, "Brother! Look at the buffalo!"

"Why do you want me to look at those buffalo?" he protested peevishly. But she insisted, and when at last he raised his head, they too fell dead. Then she skinned them and brought the hides into the brush lodge, where she spread out a few and said, "I wish these hides were tanned into fine robes." Immediately they became what she wished. Then to the other skins she addressed the same magic words, and they became soft robes decorated with paintings. Now that she had everything she needed, she built and arranged her tepee.

One day the girl saw a raven flying by, and she called

out, "Raven, take this piece of buffalo fat and go to the camp of my tribe, and when you fly over, drop it in the center of the camp circle and say, 'There is plenty to eat at the old campsite!' "

The raven took the fat and flew to the faraway camp. There he saw all the young men playing the wheel game, and dropping his burden, he croaked, "There is plenty to eat at the old campsite!" It happened that at this time there was a famine in the village, and when the words of the raven were heard, the head chief ordered some young men to go to the old camp to see what they could find. The scouts set forth, and where the old camp had been they saw a fine elk-skin lodge with racks of meat swinging in the wind and buffalo grazing on the surrounding hills. When the chief heard their report, he immediately told his crier to give the order to break camp.

When a new camp had been made near the elk-skin tepee, the father and the mother of the girl quickly discovered that it belonged to their daughter, and they went to her, calling, "My daughter! My daughter!" But she answered, "Keep back! You are not my father, and you are not my mother, for when I found the lodge poles and cried out to you not to leave me, you went on, saying that I was no daughter of yours!"

After a while, however, she seemed to forgive them, and calling all the people around her, she divided among them a large quantity of boiled buffalo tongues. She asked her parents to sit by her side. Meanwhile, her brother had been sitting with his head bowed.

Suddenly the girl cried, "Brother, look at these people! They are the ones who deserted us!"

She repeated her words twice, but the boy would not look up. At the fourth command he raised his head slowly, and as he looked around, the people fell lifeless.

Then the girl said, "Let a few of the men and women return to life, so that the tribe may grow again, but let their characters be changed. Let the people be better than they were." Immediately some of them came to life, and the tribe increased, and their hearts were good.

*"the tribe increased, and their
hearts were good"*

Fox and the Bears

Two bears were brothers, living in a place not far from
here. One of them was sick, it seems, and very close to
death, and the other one was doing all he could to save
him. He sang, he made medicine, but his poor brother,
instead of feeling better, felt only worse. He howled with
pain. Well, Fox heard about it and came around to see
what he could do, and he doctored and he doctored, but in
spite of everything, Bear died.

"He howled with pain."

Well, as they were about to bury the body, Fox said, "Don't bury it in the ground. It would be better to just . . . drop it in the water!"

Then Fox went home and told his children to go downstream and when they saw Bear floating by to haul him out of the water and bring him home. So they did, and it wasn't long before Fox and his family were having a nice feast.

While they were eating, a little bird came down and asked for some food. But they wouldn't give him any. The bird said, "I know who you're eating. And if you don't give me some, I'll go tell that other bear what you did with his brother's body."

"Go ahead. Tell all you know."

The bird flew away, and Fox began to get scared. He hid all the meat. Then he looked at his children and thought for a minute. Well, then, this is what he did. He cut all their fur off, then he covered himself with ashes, and they all started to wail.

Soon the other bear came along and stopped and watched. He watched for a long, long time. Then he said to himself, "Their hearts are true. They are mourning for my poor dead brother."

So the bear went away. And as soon as he was out of sight, Fox and his children went over to where they'd buried the meat and dug it up again. It looked pretty good, and they kept on eating until it was all gone.

From the North Woods

*Among the lakes and forests of central Canada lived a widely
scattered people who made their homes in tepees and used
birchbark canoes. In this country it was the custom for a
married woman, if she wished, to take a second husband. The
man of her choice would be expected to give her first husband
one or more horses and continue to offer him gifts from time
to time. The two men then considered themselves "comrades,"
or "brothers." But if a woman took a second husband
secretly, without payment, her first husband, if he caught her,
would punish her severely. In the tale called "The Woman
Dressed Like a Man" such a wife is put to death. This story is
from the Cree of Saskatchewan.*

The Woman Dressed Like a Man

A woman once had two small sons. She was married to a brave warrior. But she fell in love with another man, who was younger, and they would meet secretly as often as they could. One day the young man said to her, "I wish we could always be together."

"That would be easy to do," she answered.

"How could we do it?"

"Well, I will pretend to be sick and die. Then you can

come and get me and we will go away."

So they arranged it.

The woman pretended to be very ill. She ate nothing and became thin. The medicine men could do nothing for her. At last she called her husband and said, "I feel I am going to die. When I die, you must go away at once, for I do not wish my parents and my brothers to grieve for me." Then she pretended to die. They wrapped her in a skin, tied it with rope, and placed her on a platform in a tree. As soon as this was done, they moved away.

In the night her lover came. "Are you alive?" he called.

"Yes! Cut the rope and take me out. I'm hungry."

He cut the rope and fed her, and they traveled far away. The woman wore her hair like a man and put on man's clothing. They practiced singing together, and when she had learned to sing like a man, they went back to their people.

The young man told his family that he had been visiting far in the south and had brought home a chum; and they were pleased. The two were constantly together. They would go down to the place where the girls got water, in order to make people think they were both young men looking for sweethearts.

One day the woman's two little boys came for water. She was filled with longing to speak to them and to hear their voices. She said, "Little boys, give me a drink." The older boy gave her the pail. She drank, and gave it back and laughed. Now, when she laughed she had a dimple in each cheek. The boy looked closely at her. He recognized his mother, but said nothing. He went home, and said to his father, "Father, I have seen my mother."

"My little son, don't say that!" The man took him in his arms and cried. Then he said, "My boy, never say that. Your mother has gone away. She is dead. Never say that. Don't say it to your grandmother and make her sad."

So the boy said nothing more. But a few days later he went again for water, and again the woman asked for a drink. Once more he noticed the dimples and was sure it was his mother. He went home and told his father what he had seen, and this time his father listened, but told him to say nothing to the others.

Early in the morning, the father got on his horse and

rode to the place where they had left the body of his wife. He saw that the skin was empty and that the rope had been cut with a knife. He returned and said to his son, "Go to your grandmother and ask her for two dishes of serviceberry soup." The boy did so, and soon returned with the dishes.

Then the father sent his son to invite the two who were constantly together. When they arrived, he placed the man at his left and the woman at the man's left. He fed them the soup, then gave a large pipe to the young man. The man smoked and passed the pipe to the woman. But she had not learned to use tobacco, and when she inhaled she began to cough, and the sound was that of a woman's cough. Instantly her lover leaped up and ran out of the tepee. She tried to follow, but her husband grasped her by the hair and forced her to sit down. He had a long knife, and he was a warrior. She was afraid to resist.

The husband then sent his older son to call his grandparents and his five uncles. When they came in and sat down, he said, "My father-in-law, you thought your daughter was dead. This morning I went to the place

"She said, 'Little boys, give me a drink.' "

where we left her. The skin was empty and the rope cut with a knife. There sits your daughter. Look closely and you will recognize her. Now what do you think of her?"

The old man looked closely and saw that it was so. He said, "I thought my daughter was a woman, but I find that she is an animal. I do not want to see her. I thought she was dead. Let her remain dead." He got up and went out. His wife followed, and one by one their five sons departed. The woman's husband reached for his knife and killed her.

The young lover disappeared. He intended to let the Blackfeet kill him. That would be better than dying at the hands of his own people. One day as he was picking serviceberries, he saw three people on horseback. He hid among the bushes, and when they came close he saw an old woman, a middle-aged woman, and a girl. They tied their horses and separated to pick berries. The two older women were close to his hiding place. He made a noise like a grizzly bear, and they were frightened. He seized one and plunged his knife into her, then the other. The young girl was running for the horses, but he overtook her. He said by signs: "Do not fear. I will not harm you." He scalped the two older women, placed the girl on one of the horses, mounted another, and drove the third ahead, riding rapidly to escape being chased.

At night he built a small shelter. He said to the girl: "You will sleep here. I will sleep there."

She was surprised and asked in signs: "Why do we not sleep together?"

"I did not take you for my wife," he said. "When we get home you will be the wife of my brother."

It was late the next day when they got back to camp. The young man told the girl to make herself clean and paint her face. Then he led her to the tepee of the man he had wronged, and by signs told her to go in and sit beside the man she would find there. This she did. The man was surprised, but said nothing. Then the young man went in. He sat down opposite the other man and said, "My brother, I did something very bad to you. But take this woman. And here is something more for you." He gave him the two scalps. "Outside are three horses. They are yours. There is one thing more: I give you my body. Do with it what you will." He bowed his head.

"Then the young man went in."

The other raised him up and said, "My brother, say not so. I will not harm you. It is true you did something very bad to me, but today you have done something very good. From now on you shall be my real brother."

From the Southwest

The spectacular desert landscapes of Arizona and New Mexico have religious significance for the tribes who make this region their home. The land itself is regarded as sacred, and many of its features — mountains, canyons, and springs — are holy places. The myth called "The Dirty Bride," from the Hopi of Arizona, tells how one of these holy places came into existence. The story that follows it is a sacred narrative of the Navajo. It explains how the land in its entirety was made safe in the ancient days by the twin heroes Monster-Slayer and Child-of-the-Water.

The Dirty Bride

Long ago, in a village that now lies in ruins, there lived a young man who would get up each morning before sunrise and practice running. Each day he would make an offering to the gods in order to become swift and strong. Otherwise, day and night, he remained in his house. He never went down to the stream where the young women gathered. Although he was handsome, he had no sweetheart. His name was Rainbow Boy.

*"Each day he would make an
offering to the gods"*

One day he let it be known that he would stay unmarried for the rest of his life, unless he found a girl who could grind cornmeal so fine that it would stick to the surface of a beautiful abalone shell that hung on the wall in his house.

Then all the girls in the surrounding villages began to grind meal, making it as fine as possible. For they all wished to marry this handsome boy.

A girl from one of the more distant villages was the first to come for the trial. Rainbow Boy was kind and courteous to her. He invited her into his house, and after a while he asked, "What is it you wish?"

"I have come for you," she answered.

"Very well," said the boy. He opened a cloth that contained the girl's meal and threw some of it against the shell, but it did not stick. "I cannot go with you and be your husband," he said. "Your meal does not stick to my shell."

"Very well," answered the girl quietly, and she departed.

Soon another young woman arrived, and another, and another. But each in turn failed to pass the test.

Now in a village quite nearby there lived a girl named

*"they all wished to marry this
handsome boy"*

Corn Smut, whose face was smeared with dirt. Her brothers told her that they did not think Rainbow Boy would consent to come with her, even if her meal should stick to the shell. Nevertheless, she said she would try. Then she took some of her meal and went to the young man's house. He invited her to enter and sit down, and he asked what she wished.

"I have come for you," she said.

"Very well," he answered. He took some of the meal and threw it against the shell, and it stuck fast. "Very well," he said. "It is my word. I have agreed to marry the girl whose meal stuck to my shell, and your meal has done so. Therefore I will go with you. I will live in your house and be your husband." So they went to the house of Corn Smut.

Her brothers and her mother were surprised. They were also pleased. Toward evening, however, the girl went into an adjoining room and did not return. Then, unexpectedly, from out of the same room came a beautiful young woman, and Rainbow Boy wondered who she could be.

About bedtime the brothers began to speak to her as though nothing unusual had happened, and the boy then

"she revealed her true self"

understood that the beautiful young woman was none other than their sister and his bride. Her dirty appearance had been due to a mask that she wore during the day. Every day she wore the mask, but at night she revealed her true self.

Now the other girls, who had been rejected, were angry and made fun of Rainbow Boy and his dirty bride. But the young man did not mind, because he knew that his wife was really beautiful. And so they lived on, happily, for some time.

But this strange bride was a supernatural being, and one day she announced to her husband that she would have to leave the world of humans. Shortly thereafter she and all her family disappeared into the ground. The spot where she disappeared is now the shrine called Place of the Corn Smut Girl, a holy place where people come to make prayers.

How the World Was Saved

The first people were created inside the earth. When the time came for them to emerge, they crawled up into the sunlight and lived on the surface. But they were afraid.

In those days the world was ruled by man-eating birds, giant animals, and other monsters, who seized people and devoured them or crushed them to death. Each year more people were lost. Their numbers grew smaller and smaller.

One day, on a mountain slope near the center of the

world, a baby girl appeared, brought forth as the daughter of earth and sky. She was found on the mountain by First Man, who had been the first person to emerge from inside the earth. First Man took the baby with him to his home. He cared for her, and there she matured in just twelve days, becoming a beautiful woman with supernatural powers. Shortly thereafter she went to live in a home of her own at the foot of the mountain where she had been born. She was now called White-Shell Woman.

In the morning this woman would lie on the eastern slope of the mountain until the sun rose high in the sky. Then, when the day grew warm, she would go down to a stream and seek the shade of jutting rocks, allowing droplets of water to trickle over her body.

Before long she gave birth to twin boys, never realizing that it had been the sunlight and dripping water that had made her pregnant. The older boy, the one born first, would come to be known as Monster-Slayer. His younger brother was Child-of-the-Water. Like their mother, the boys matured quickly, and in a matter of days they were nearly grown.

*"when the day grew warm, she would
go down to a stream"*

At that time the giants and monsters were rapidly destroying the few remaining people. To protect her sons, White-Shell Woman kept them hidden away on the mountainside. But the two boys begged to be free, and at last their mother allowed them to play about, warning them, however, to stay close to home.

The boys promised to obey, and for a while they did. But one day they asked their mother to tell them who their father was, and because she said she did not know, they became angry, broke their promise, and wandered off toward the east. They intended to find someone who could tell them what they wanted to know.

As they traveled along, they heard a whispered "Sh-h."

"Are you afraid, my younger brother?" asked the older twin.

"No!" was the quick reply.

Four times they heard the whisper. It was Wind. "I saw you traveling eastward," he said, "and came to warn you. The land is cursed with monsters who kill for pleasure. Beware of them! Why do you journey alone like this without your father?"

" 'Are you afraid, my younger brother?' "

"Our father? We know nothing of him. Do you know who he is?" asked the boys.

"Yes, the Sun is your father. But if you want to find him, you will have to travel far eastward and cross the wide, wide waters."

The older boy turned to his brother and said, "Let us go."

Because they were sacred beings, the boys covered distances rapidly, and by midafternoon they had passed well beyond the limits of their homeland. Traveling on through strange country, they came upon an old woman, who sat beside a ladder leading downward into a hole. She asked them who they were and where they were going. They answered, saying, "We are going to see our father, the Sun."

"My grandchildren, I pity you," she said. "Come in and rest a moment before going on." She started down the ladder and the boys followed. The old woman was Spider Woman, the little grandmother who belongs to the gods.

Her home was well kept, clean, and comfortable, and the boys were glad to rest. "My grandchildren," she said, "your journey is long, and many dangers will beset you before you reach the end. Take these life feathers. They will help you. If difficulties befall you, use them," and she gave each boy two feathers plucked from a living eagle.

They took the feathers, thanked the old woman, and continued their journey. After traveling a while, they came to a ridge of loose sand. They tried to climb it but could not. Each time they tried, the sand gave way. Then they remembered the sacred feathers, and putting them on their feet, they easily crossed the ridge.

Next they came to four rows of tall, thorny reeds that parted and closed without warning. The boys walked boldly up to the reeds and started in, then jumped back quickly. The reeds closed at once, but did not catch them. Then they put the life feathers on their feet again and leaped over all four rows.

Next they came to a deep canyon with straight walls, and after that a narrow passage through shifting rocks that would open, then crash together. But both times the boys used their life feathers and continued on without harm.

Soon they reached a great sheet of water, stretching as far as the eye could see. Again they used their life feathers and were carried safely over. Four stretches of water were crossed, one after another, and still a fifth sheet of water lay before them. They stood for a moment and gazed.

In the center of the water, deep in the distance, they could see a house of turquoise and white shell. Its roof glistened in the sunlight. Certain that this must be the home of their father, they attempted to cross over. But this time they found that their life feathers were of no use. They tried again and again, but without success.

The thought of not reaching their father's house after having come so far filled them with bitter disappointment. As they sat in silence, wondering what to do, a little old man came up to them and asked, "Where are you going, my grandchildren?" It was Snipe Man who spoke.

"To the home of the Sun," the boys replied.

"Do you know anyone there?"

"Yes, the Sun is our father."

Then the little old man placed a rainbow bridge across the water and told them to continue on. Crossing over the bridge, they came at last to the entrance of the great house, but there before them were bears, lightning, snakes, and wind, barring their way. To each they spoke the words, "I am the child of White-Shell Woman," and they were permitted to enter.

When they reached the inner rooms of the house, they were met by an elderly woman, radiantly beautiful, and two boys and two girls more handsome than anyone they had ever seen. These were the wife of the Sun and her four children. At first the woman was angry. But when she thought of what her husband might do when he came home and found strangers in his house, her anger turned to pity and she wrapped the boys up in the clouds that hung on the western wall.

Soon a great rattle was heard outside. A moment later the Sun came striding in and hung up his glistening shield. "What strangers are here?" he asked. There was no answer. Again he asked, and again and again, growing angrier each time. Still no answer. The Sun looked about, and noticing a change in the clouds on the wall, took them down, unfolded them, and discovered the two boys.

Now he was angrier than ever and determined to kill the strangers. Around the walls on all four sides were jeweled spikes. The boys were hurled against the east wall, the south wall, the west wall, and finally the north wall, but each time they dropped to the floor unhurt. Then they were placed on huge grinding stones and pounded to bits — or so their father thought. But again they were unhurt. Next the Sun handed them each two pipes of tobacco, saying, "I wish you to have a good smoke."

"Beware!" whispered the Wind. "His tobacco is poisoned." But the boys, once again, were not harmed.

Dismayed, the Sun called out to the Fire God. The boys felt warm. They laid down their pipes and looked up, and there before them stood the Fire God. The Sun ordered him to build a sweat bath and to fill it with stones as hot as he could make them. When all was ready, the boys were made to enter, and the Fire God sealed the doorway with red-hot boulders. Then their father called, "Are you warm?" They gave no answer. Four times he called, but received no answer. "I am rid of them at last," he thought. But when the boulders were pushed aside, the boys emerged unhurt as before.

"These must be my sons," cried the Sun, and he rushed

"there before them stood the Fire God"

forward and embraced them. Then he directed his wife and daughters to reshape the boys and make them as handsome as themselves. He offered them gifts of turquoise beads, and beads of abalone, white shell, and jet. But the twins refused, saying they preferred to have lightning arrows, strong bows, and heavy knives with which to battle the giants and monsters who were destroying people in all parts of the earth. The Sun gave them the weapons they desired, and when it came time for him to resume his journey across the sky, he took his newfound sons with him.

In the south lived a giant as tall as a mountain. The boys decided to try their skill on him first. As soon as they saw him, their father let them down from the sky. The giant was drinking water from a lake and saw the reflection of his new enemies as they dropped to earth. He straightened up quickly and sent an arrow aimed for the body of the older twin, but the boy dodged and sent back a bolt of lightning that stripped the armor from the giant's feet. Three more shafts of lightning struck the armor from the hips, body, and head of this fiercest of giants, exposing him fully to the attack of the boys, who now shot him with arrows, killing him instantly.

The giant's blood began to flow down a canyon. The older twin drew a line across its path with his stone knife, and the blood flowed no farther, rising in a wall across the head of the canyon. When it dried, it became a cliff, over which now plunges a beautiful waterfall.

The brothers then set off for home, taking the heart of their slain enemy with them. When they reached their mother, they found her in tears, for she thought that her sons had been devoured by the monsters. Though unchanged in size, so different were they in appearance that White-Shell Woman did not at first know who they were. But when they told the story of their adventures, she understood at last, and all were glad.

In the days that followed, they searched out and destroyed the giant antelope called Daelget, who tossed people to death with his great blue horns. Next they killed the preying Mountain Eagle, and soon after that the monster called Among-the-Rocks-He-Kicks-Them-Down-the-Mountain.

"The people were no longer afraid to travel from place to place."

Then they attacked the one called He-Kills-With-His-Eyes, then Rolling Boulder, and finally the great Tracking Bear.

At last the people were safe from the curse that had nearly destroyed the world. All the giants and great monsters had lost their lives. The people were no longer afraid to travel from place to place. They never forgot the deeds of Monster-Slayer and Child-of-the-Water, and from that time on they revered them as gods.

From Alaska

The Eskimos of Alaska, like those of Canada and Greenland, depend heavily upon the sea. Among some groups, caribou and other land animals are hunted during the summer months, but the more important sources of food are fish, seals, and small whales. Because of the uncertainty of the food supply, meat is often dried and stored, especially with the onset of winter. Many are the stories of long hard winters, of families near starvation, and of hunters who set out to sea in dangerous weather, never to return. It is with this background in mind that the following tale was told. It was collected among the Kotzebue Eskimos of northwestern Alaska.

The Lost Boys

Two boys were living with their parents in a house at the edge of the sea. While the weather was warm, the father caught fish and brought home furs and caribou meat. But summer was almost over, and soon the family would have to leave for their winter village.

When the time came, the mother went to the drying racks, took down the fish she had dried, and packed it in the family's boat. Their furs, their caribou meat, and all

"in a house at the edge of the sea"

their household belongings were put in the boat too.

When everything was loaded, the mother and father jumped ashore with the dogs and began to pull the boat along by a rope. The boys remained aboard to steer. Suddenly the rope snapped, and the boat, with the two boys still in it, began drifting out to sea. The boys seized paddles and tried frantically to row toward the beach, but a brisk wind kept driving them seaward, while their anguished parents, helpless, stood waving their arms on the shore.

In order to lighten the boat and make paddling easier, the boys threw all their belongings and most of their food overboard. But this only raised the boat higher out of the water, allowing the wind to push it more swiftly.

The older boy pretended he wasn't afraid. He comforted his little brother and told him not to cry. Night came, there was fog, and the wind blew them farther and farther away.

For days they were blown about. Often storms arose, threatening to swamp the boat. During a long period of foggy weather, they gave up all hope. But one night, while sleeping exhaustedly, they were awakened by the sound of the boat pounding on the bottom.

In the morning, when the fog cleared, the brothers found they had drifted to shore. Before them stretched a low, flat country, and close to the beach there was a strange village and many people. The younger boy wanted to go up to them at once, thinking they might be friendly. But his brother warned him, "No, we must be careful. These people are strangers."

They landed quietly and slipped across the beach without being noticed.

Close by were women cutting meat. Other people were lighting cooking fires. Men were dragging home seals, and there were drying racks hung with fish. The boys were hungry. But they did not dare to let themselves be seen.

Instead, they hid in the graveyard on the far side of the village. There among the grave-posts they waited until it was dark. Then they slipped up to the houses and stole food. Next day they did the same, and the next day after that.

The following day they found a small storehouse built on a raised platform. It was where the people of the village kept their dried meat, so that it would be safe from wild

"Close by were women cutting meat."

animals. When no one was looking, the boys stole some of the meat. The next day they came back for more. And in this way they kept from starving. But at last after many days, the villagers began to wonder who was stealing their food. They grew angry.

One day, when the people had gathered for a feast, the brothers overheard them talking about the stolen food. Perhaps birds or wild animals had discovered their storage place. No one knew for sure.

A medicine man was called. The people asked him to use his power to find out who the thieves might be. The man beat his drum and sang loudly, then announced: "I can learn nothing. There are no strange animals here, only humans. Humans must have stolen your food. Perhaps there are strangers nearby."

Then a second medicine man was called. His power was very great. He cried aloud: "Your food is being stolen by two persons. They are over there!" Then the people noticed the brothers. But at first they could not believe that so much food had been stolen by two children. And so once again they called for help.

This time it was a medicine woman who came. She was old, and her power was the greatest of all. She ordered the people to go back to their houses. When they had left, she said to the boys, "Come! My spirit powers tell me I must take you with me. I will protect you and give you food."

The entranceway to her home was well lighted and crowded with dried foods and hunting equipment of all kinds. There she bathed the brothers and dressed them in fine clothing. When they were bathed and clothed, she led them into the house itself, which was decorated with many strings of beads and had fine beds of caribou skins. They were each instructed to choose a bead, and these were strung with smaller beads and given to them to wear as headbands.

The brothers were kept inside until they were nearly grown. They became strong young men and learned athletic games, but they were not allowed to leave the house except late at night or when the villagers had gone away on a hunting trip.

No one knew that the old medicine woman had raised the two boys. But one day, when they disobeyed her and

"her power was the greatest of all"

"and dressed them in fine clothing"

went outside, a medicine man saw them. Soon a messenger appeared at the smoke hole. The old woman asked, "What do you want here?"

"The medicine man wants you and the two young men to come to the center of the village. You must all dress in your finest clothing, because you are about to die."

When they were ready, the messenger made the woman and the two brothers follow him to the shore, where a seal hunter stood poised with a harpoon. But just as the hunter was about to turn and kill them, the old woman used her magic, and the hunter was paralyzed. She would not let him move until the people came and brought her food and other gifts.

A second time the medicine man sent a messenger. And again a hunter stood poised, then turned to kill them. But he too was paralyzed by the old woman's power. Then again the people were forced to bring gifts.

And yet a third time the people tried to kill the boys. And again they were made to bring gifts, until at last there were many sealskin bags filled with food, clothing, and other valuables, lying in a row beside the old woman's house.

In the fall of that year the medicine woman called the messenger to her and said, "These boys are now grown men, and it is time for them to visit their parents. They are the ones who stole food from the storehouse long ago. They must be allowed to go about the village now. You and the others who have tried to do us harm must build a large boat-frame this winter. In the spring it must be provided with a skin cover and loaded with food and rich gifts of all kinds.

In the spring, when the boat was ready to be launched, the men pushed it into the water. Then they loaded all the food and gifts and raised the sail.

The two young men and the old woman got into the boat, taking the messenger along with them to be their pilot. A wind blew up, and soon they were on their way.

After a long journey, they reached the village where the boys' parents were living. The mother and father recognized their children at once and were filled with joy at the sight of them.

The old woman was joyful too, for she recognized the boys' father as her son. Then the boys knew that the old woman was their grandmother. The family remained to-gether for the rest of the summer and throughout the long winter. When spring came again, the grandmother's boat was piled with food and many presents. Then, taking the pilot with her, she set sail and returned to her own country.

A Note About the Making of This Book

Unusual care has been taken in the reproduction of the photographs included in this edition. The work was done in Philadelphia by Pearl Pressman Liberty. As a preliminary step, press proofs were run using plates prepared with a variety of camera techniques and inked to match the original Curtis gravures in the collection of The University of Pennsylvania Museum—using different papers. The final photo-offset plates were prepared by a triple-dot process and printed on Perkins and Squier offset vellum. Each picture requires two plates, one inked in brown, the other in black. Of the twenty-eight photographs that appear in this book, fourteen were taken from gravures owned by The University of Pennsylvania Museum, the remaining fourteen from gravures owned by The Philadelphia Museum of Art. Although most of the pictures are from the twenty bound volumes of *The North American Indian* (NA), several are from the accompanying looseleaf portfolios (NAP). The picture sources are as follows: pp. 83, 91, and 94 (NA, vol. I); p. 47 (NA, vol. IV); p. 55 (NA, vol. V); p. 37 (NA, vol. VIII); p. 19 (NA, vol. IX); pp. 6, 10, 27, and 29 (NA, vol. X); pp. 7 and 15 (NA, vol. XI); pp. ii, 100, 103, 106, and 107 (NA, vol. XX); pp. 85, 52–3, 22–3, 76–7, 79, 40, 74, 65, 68, and 46 (NAP, plates 32, 207, 302, 400, 406, 454, 586, 622, 624, and 637, respectively).

Story sources: "The Girl Who Married a Ghost" (NA, vol. IX, pp. 129—34), "The Dance of the Spirit Monster" (NA, vol. X, pp. 296—8), "Asleep-by-the-Stream" (NA, vol. XIII, pp. 197—8), "The Deserted Children" (NA, vol. V, pp. 127—30), "Fox and the Bears" (NA, vol. XIX, pp. 191—2), "The Woman Dressed Like a Man" (NA, vol. XVIII, pp. 133—4), "The Dirty Bride" (NA, vol. XII, pp. 198—9), "How the World Was Saved" (NA, vol. I, pp. 98—106), "The Lost Boys" (NA, vol. XX, pp. 179—81).

Stories, captions, and all display type have been set in ITC Zapf International Medium, a new face designed by the well-known typographer Hermann Zapf.

Books By and About Edward Curtis

Andrews, Ralph W., *Curtis' Western Indians*, Bonanza Books, N.Y., 1962. A short but informative biography, illustrated with very poor reproductions of Curtis's photographs.

Boesen, Victor, and Graybill, Florence Curtis, *Edward S. Curtis: Photographer of the North American Indian*, Dodd, Mead, N.Y., 1977. A biography for young readers, illustrated.

Curtis, Edward S., *The North American Indian*, 20 vols. + 20 looseleaf portfolios, Cambridge, Mass. (vols. 1–5) and Norwood, Mass. (vols. 6–20), 1907–30. A limited edition of 500 sets; reprinted 1970, 2nd printing 1974, by Johnson Reprint Co., N.Y.

————, *Indian Days of the Long Ago,* World Book Co., Yonkers, 1914. A small book of lore and legend, illustrated with photographs. Reprinted by Tamarack Press, 1975.

————, *In the Land of the Head Hunters,* World Book Co., Yonkers, 1915. A fictionalized account of the Kwakiutl Indians of British Columbia, illustrated with photographs. Reprinted by Tamarack Press, 1975.

————, *The Sioux and the Apsaroke, From Volumes Three and Four of The North American Indian,* ed. by Stuart Zoll, foreword by A.D. Coleman, Harper and Row, N.Y., 1975.

————, *Portraits from North American Indian Life,* introductions by A.D. Coleman and T.C. McLuhan, Outerbridge and Lazard, N.Y., 1972, reprinted by Promontory Press. An excellent, large-format portfolio. Curtis's pictures are well reproduced.

Fowler, Don D., and Homer, Rachel J., *In a Sacred Manner We Live: Photographs of the North American Indian by Edward S. Curtis,* Barre Publishing, Barre, Mass., 1972. A well-edited album of Curtis's pictures, satisfactorily reproduced.

Gifford, Barry, ed., *Selected Writings of Edward S. Curtis,* Creative Arts Book Co., 1976.

Graybill, Florence Curtis, and Boesen, Victor, *Edward Sherriff Curtis: Visions of a Vanishing Race,* Thomas Y. Crowell, N.Y., 1976. A reminiscence by one of Curtis's daughters, illustrated with very poor reproductions of Curtis's photographs.

Hoffman, Michael E., ed., *The North American Indians: A Selection of Photographs by Edward S. Curtis,* introduction by Joseph Epes Brown, Aperture, N.Y., 1972. The photographs are handsomely reproduced.